Stories of Stone

Happy House

About Wise & Wide

- A systematic 6-level English reading program based on Lexile® measures
- Diverse and interesting topics chosen from the elementary curriculums of Korea and English speaking western countries
- Well-written books in various forms including fiction stories, descriptive texts, and classics retold
- The informative but original fiction stories grab your interest, leading to the easy and clear understanding of the educational content.
- Improve thinking skills with solid after-reading activities at all levels of the series.

Wise & Wide is a 6-level English reading program that consists of 60 books and each level is systematically divided by Lexile® measures. The Lexile® Framework for Reading is the most popular reading measuring system in American formal education curriculums and many English programs. Over 20 out of 50 states in the U.S. mark Lexile® measures directly on students' final report cards and over 300 well-known publishers adopt and use Lexile® measures.

Experience many kinds of readings written by professional writers from the U.S. and England. They used interesting topics that were carefully chosen after analyzing elementary curriculums from around the world including Korea, the U.S., England, and Australia among many others. Comprehensive after-reading activities including graphic organizers, speaking tasks, and After-reading Tests are ready for you.

Levels in the series and their corresponding Lexile® measures

Level	Lexile® measures	U.S. Grade
Level 1	Below 200L	Pre K - K
Level 2	190L - 400L	Lower Grade 1
Level 3	350L - 530L	Upper Grade 1
Level 4	420L - 650L	Grade 2
Level 5	520L - 940L	Grade 3 - 4
Level 6	830L - 1070L	Grade 5 - 6

* Smart Readers: Wise & Wide level 1 is applicable to the preschool level in the U.S.
* The source of the relationship between Lexile® measures and U.S. school grades: CCSS(Common Core State Standards) FOR ENGLISH LANGUAGE ARTS, APPENDIX A (2012, which is used by 45 states in the U.S.)

Topic List

	Level 1	Level 2	Level 3	Level 4	Level 5	Level 6
Book 1	Science>Biology: The hibernation of animals / Story	Science>Biology: Living and nonliving things / Story	Science>Biology> Animals & the Environment: Sea otters / Story	Environment> Living with nature: The diver & the persimmon tree / Story	Science>Biology> Animal: Amazing animals of the Amazon / Story	Science>Biology: Germs, transmitted diseases / Story
Book 2	Literature> World classics: Aesop's fables / Story	Literature> Traditional fairy tale: Old tales about stones / Story	Social Studies> Economy: To run a business to make and save money / Story	Science>Biology> Plants: Photosynthesis / Story	Science>Earth science: Earth's layers, earthquakes, volcanoes, and earth's atmosphere / Report	Mathematics> Sequence: The golden ratio & the Fibonacci sequence / Story
Book 3	Science>Physics: How shadows are formed / Story	Literature> World classics: Peter Pan / Story	Science>Scientific technology: Nanobots / Story	Literature>Myths: World's creation stories / Story	Literature> Legend: The story of King Arthur / Story	Literature>Myths: Constellation myths / Story
Book 4	Literature> Traditional literature: The Talmud / Story	Science>Biology> Animal: Polar bears / Story	Science>Biology> Animal: Mountain gorillas / Story	Social Studies> Cultural anthropology: Amazing ancient cultures of the world / Story	Science> Earth science: Clouds and weather / Story	Literature> Human & animals: The friendship between a girl and a horse / Story
Book 5	Social Studies> Ethics: Rules in daily life / Story	Science>Biology: The five senses / Report	Social Studies> Cultural anthropology: Astonishing festivals / Report	Art>Music: Stories from two operas / Story	Social Studies> World culture & history: The Renaissance / Story	Sports> Board sports: Surfing & snowboarding / Story
Book 6	Social Studies> World geography & travel: Tourist attractions around the world / Story	Science>Biology> Animal: Dinosaurs / Story	Science> Astronomy: The solar system / Story	Social Studies> People: Three great people who overcame hardships / Story	Science>Scientific technology: The wonderful world of robots / Report	Art>Music: Composers of the Romantic Era / Report
Book 7	Science> Space science: The life of astronauts / Report	Social Studies> Cultural anthropology: Mythological monsters from around the world / Report	Mathematics> Elementary mathematics: Numbers, measurement, shapes and data / Report	Science & Social Studies> Technology & culture: Inventions from around the world / Report	Art>Works of art: Famous paintings / Report	Social Studies> Human & animals: Animals in action for human / Report
Book 8	Social Studies> Cultural anthropology: Various living cultures of the world / Story	Art>Music: Instruments in the orchestra / Story	Social Studies> Life safety: Learning and using outdoor survival skills / Story	Social Studies> History: The California Gold Rush / Report	Social Studies & Science> Psychology: Psychology in everyday life / Story	Literature> World classics: The Merchant of Venice / Story
Book 9	Social Studies> Jobs: Interviews about jobs / Report	Science>Scientific technology: Developments in technology in different times / Story	Social Studies> Politics>Election: Running for 3rd grade class president / Story	Literature> World classics: Stories of Sherlock Holmes / Story	Literature> World classics: Adrift in the Pacific / Story	Social Studies> History & People: Great world leaders in history / Report
Book 10	Literature>Traditional fairy tale: Eastern and Western folk tales on the same theme / Story	Sports>Winter sports: Various aspects of some Winter Olympic sports / Report	Literature> World classics: Short stories by O. Henry / Story	Sports> Ball games: Various aspects of popular ball games / Report	Social Studies> History: Famous events that changed world history / Report	Art & Social Studies> Art: Stories about the creation, distribution, and preservation of paintings / Report

How to Use This Book

• Before Reading

You can easily find the topic and what kind of story you are about to read.

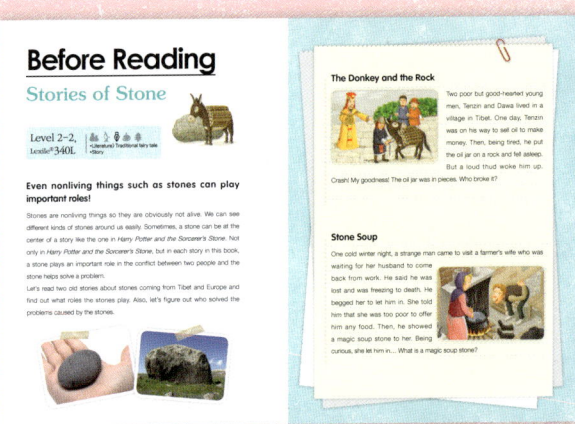

• The text

All the stories were written by professional writers from the U.S. and England, so you will read authentic and appropriate English sentences and expressions in every book in the series.

• Pop Quiz

Check out right away if you understand what you have just read by solving a pop quiz that checks your comprehension.

• Key Words

The key words and expressions on each page are listed for you to easily study them.

• Aha! Tips

Download free Korean explanations at *www.ihappyhouse.co.kr* for all of the sentences marked with "Aha!". These explain cultural, scientific, and economic knowledge or they deal with aspects of English such as grammatical structures or idiomatic expressions. There are lots of "Aha! Tips" to help you understand the text.

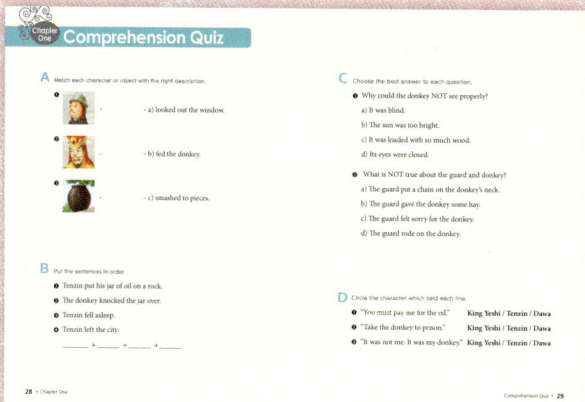

• Comprehension Quiz

After reading one chapter, solve various questions to find out if you fully understand the content.

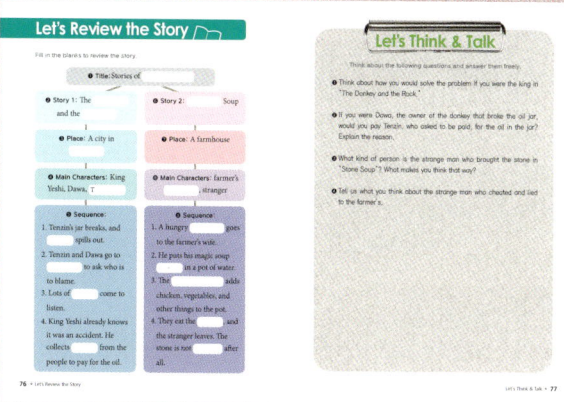

• Let's Review the Story /
• Let's Think & Talk

Fill in the blanks in the organizer to summarize the whole story. Express your own thinking and feelings about the story by answering the questions. You can build up logic and reasoning skills for your essay examinations in the future.

Appendix

Audio Files
The texts are read vividly by American professional voice actors.
(Audio files downloaded for free)

After-reading Test
Solve an additionally provided After-reading Test for each book.

The Korean translation, Answer Keys, a Word Quiz, a Word List, and Aha! Tips for each book
You can download them for free at *www.ihappyhouse.co.kr*

Before Reading

Stories of Stone

Level 2-2, Lexile® 340L

• Literature)Traditional Fairy Tale
• Story

Even nonliving things such as stones can play important roles!

Stones are nonliving things so they are obviously not alive. We can see different kinds of stones around us easily. Sometimes, a stone can be at the center of a story like the one in *Harry Potter and the Sorcerer's Stone*. Not only in *Harry Potter and the Sorcerer's Stone*, but in each story in this book, a stone plays an important role in the conflict between two people and the stone helps solve a problem.

Let's read two old stories about stones coming from Tibet and Europe and find out what roles the stones play. Also, let's figure out who solved the problems caused by the stones.

The Donkey and the Rock

Two poor but good-hearted young men, Tenzin and Dawa lived in a village in Tibet. One day, Tenzin was on his way to sell oil to make money. Then, being tired, he put the oil jar on a rock and fell asleep. But a loud thud woke him up.

Crash! My goodness! The oil jar was in pieces. Who broke it?

Stone Soup

One cold winter night, a strange man came to visit a farmer's wife who was waiting for her husband to come back from work. He said he was lost and was freezing to death. He begged her to let him in. She told him that she was too poor to offer him any food. Then, he showed a magic soup stone to her. Being

curious, she let him in… What is a magic soup stone?

Contents

Stories of Stone

The Donkey
and the Rock

The Broken Jar

A long time ago, there lived a king.

His name was Yeshi.

Yeshi lived in the land of Tibet, where there were lots of mountains. Aha!

King Yeshi lived in a city that was high on a mountain.

He lived near the sky.

King Yeshi ruled the land.

He was very wise, and his people loved him.

▲ Tibet

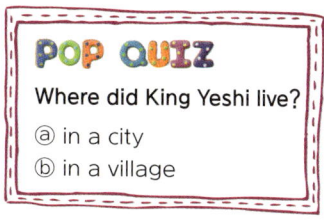

POP QUIZ

Where did King Yeshi live?

ⓐ in a city
ⓑ in a village

KEY WORDS

- broken
- jar
- a long time ago
- land

- lots of
- mountain
- near
- rule

- wise
- people

In the city where Yeshi lived, there were two men.

Their names were Tenzin and Dawa.

These men were very poor.

They had no money, but they were kind and good.

They always told the truth.

Each man lived with his mother.

The men took care of their mothers.

One day, Tenzin left the city.

He took a big jar of oil with him.

He set off to walk to a village.

On the way, he sold oil to the people he met.

After a while, Tenzin grew tired.

He sat down at the side of the road for a rest.

He put his jar of oil on a large rock.

Tenzin yawned, and his eyes began to close.

At last, he fell asleep. **Aha!**

KEY WORDS

- men
- poor
- kind
- tell the truth (tell-told-told)
- each
- take care of (take-took-taken)
- one day

- leave (leave-left-left)
- take
- a jar of
- set off (set-set-set)
- on the way
- sell (sell-sold-sold)
- after a while

- grow tired (grow-grew-grown)
- rest
- put (put-put-put)
- yawn
- begin (begin-began-begun)
- close
- at last

Dawa came along the road with his donkey.

The donkey was loaded with wood.

There was so much wood that the donkey could
not see properly.

It did not see Tenzin or the jar of oil.

The donkey came too close to the rock.

It knocked the jar over.

The jar fell off the rock, and it smashed to pieces.

The oil spilled all over the road.

▲ donkey

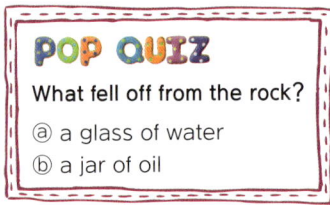

POP QUIZ

What fell off from the rock?

ⓐ a glass of water

ⓑ a jar of oil

KEY WORDS

- come along the road (come-came-come)
- donkey
- be loaded with
- properly
- knock over
- fall off (fall-fell-fallen)
- smash to pieces
- spill
- all over the road

Tenzin opened his eyes.

He saw Dawa and the donkey.

He saw the broken jar and the oil all over the road.

He was very angry.

"Look what you have done!" he shouted.

"Now I have no oil to sell."

"It was not me," said Dawa.

KEY WORDS

- shout
- pay (pay-paid-paid)
- buy (buy-bought-bought)

- feed (feed-fed-fed)
- shake one's head
  (shake-shook-shaken)

- upset
- nothing
- wrong

"It was my donkey."

"You must pay me for the oil," said Tenzin.

"No, I will not," said Dawa.

"You must!" said Tenzin.

"I have no money to buy food.

How will I feed my mother?"

But Dawa shook his head.

"I can see you are upset, but I won't pay you," he said.

"I have done nothing wrong."

The two men could not agree whose fault it was that the jar was broken.

"We must go to see King Yeshi," they said.

Dawa led his donkey down the road.

Tenzin picked up the broken pieces of his jar.

He followed Dawa and the donkey all the way back to the city.

KEY WORDS

- agree
- whose
- fault

- lead (lead-led-led)
- pick up
- piece

- follow
- all the way

They went to the king's palace and stood at the gate.

The king's guard stood in their way.

"Let us in!" said Tenzin.

"We must see the king."

"Why do you want to see him?" asked the guard.

"My jar of oil is broken," said Tenzin.

"Dawa did it."

"No, I did not," said Dawa.

"You must have done it."

The two men began to shout at each other. Aha!

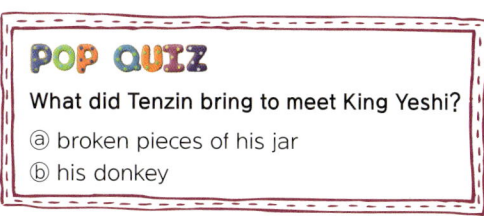

POP QUIZ

What did Tenzin bring to meet King Yeshi?
ⓐ broken pieces of his jar
ⓑ his donkey

KEY WORDS

- palace
- gate
- guard

- stand in one's way (stand-stood-stood)
- let in (let-let-let)
- each other

"Stop!" yelled the guard. Aha!

"King Yeshi will see you.

But you must not bring the donkey in here."

King Yeshi heard the loud shouting.

He looked out the window and saw the men at the gate.

"What is going on?" he called.

The men became quiet.

They did not want to make the king angry.

"These men want to see you," said the guard.

"Then let them in," said the king.

"But they want to bring the donkey into the palace," said the guard.

KEY WORDS

- yell
- bring in (bring-brought-brought)
- loud
- shouting
- look out
- call
- become (become-became-become)

King Yeshi looked at the donkey.

He did not want it to come inside the palace.

"Wait there," he said.

"I will go out to see you."

King Yeshi went to the gate.

"Now, tell me what is wrong," he said.

Tenzin spoke first.

He began to tell the king about the jar of oil.

"Now I have no oil to sell," he said.

"If I have no oil, I will make no money.

And if I have no money, I cannot feed my mother.

I have done nothing wrong.

Dawa must pay for the oil."

The king looked at Dawa.

"Did you break the jar?" he asked.

Dawa shook his head.

"No, I didn't.

The jar fell off the rock when my donkey bumped it.

But I did not touch the jar.

I have done nothing wrong."

POP QUIZ

What did Tenzin sell to make money?

ⓐ oil

ⓑ a donkey

King Yeshi nodded. "I see," he said. "Tenzin did not break the jar because he was asleep.

Dawa did not break the jar because he did not go near the rock."

"So whose fault was it?" asked the men together.

"I know you are both good men," said the king. "You always tell the truth. Aha!

If you did not do it, then it must have been the donkey or the rock.

One of them made the jar fall."

KEY WORDS

- nod
- because
- both
- chain
- around

The king called his guard.

"Put a chain around the donkey's neck," he said.

So the guard put a chain around the donkey's neck.

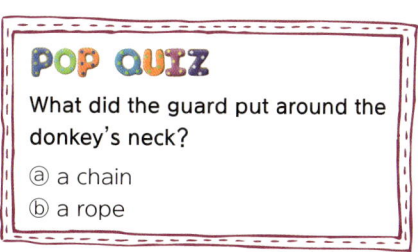

POP QUIZ

What did the guard put around the donkey's neck?

ⓐ a chain

ⓑ a rope

"Take the donkey to prison," said the king.

"What? Donkeys do not go to prison," said the guard.

"This one does," said the king.

"Take it to prison at once.

But be gentle with it.

It has worked hard, and it is tired."

The guard led the donkey away.

He tied it to a post outside the prison.

But he felt sorry for the donkey.

So he gave it some hay to eat.

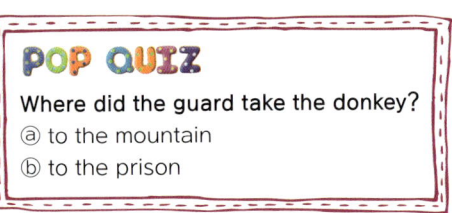

POP QUIZ

Where did the guard take the donkey?
ⓐ to the mountain
ⓑ to the prison

KEY WORDS

- go to prison
- at once
- be gentle with

- work hard
- lead away
- tie

- post
- outside
- hay

Comprehension Quiz

A Match each character or object with the right description.

· a) looked out the window.

· b) fed the donkey.

· c) smashed to pieces.

B Put the sentences in order.

❶ Tenzin put his jar of oil on a rock.

❷ The donkey knocked the jar over.

❸ Tenzin fell asleep.

❹ Tenzin left the city.

_____ → _____ → _____ → _____

C Choose the best answer to each question.

❶ Why could the donkey NOT see properly?

a) It was blind.

b) The sun was too bright.

c) It was loaded with so much wood.

d) Its eyes were closed.

❷ What is NOT true about the guard and donkey?

a) The guard put a chain on the donkey's neck.

b) The guard gave the donkey some hay.

c) The guard felt sorry for the donkey.

d) The guard rode on the donkey.

D Circle the character who said each line.

❶ "You must pay me for the oil." **King Yeshi / Tenzin / Dawa**

❷ "Take the donkey to prison." **King Yeshi / Tenzin / Dawa**

❸ "It was not me. It was my donkey." **King Yeshi / Tenzin / Dawa**

Nobody's Fault

King Yeshi called some more guards.

"I need five strong men," he said.

The five biggest, strongest men stepped forward.

"There is a large rock on the mountain road,"
said the king.

"I want you to go and find it.

Bring it to me.

I will see who broke the jar of oil.

Was it the donkey's fault, or was the rock to
blame?"

KEY WORDS

- nobody
- need
- biggest

- strongest
- step forward
- find (find-found-found)

- be to blame
- march

Tenzin and Dawa looked at each other.

"Has the king gone mad?" they said. Aha!

"How can the rock be to blame?"

The five strong men left the city.

They marched up the road.

POP QUIZ

Who did the king send to fetch the rock?

ⓐ five strong men
ⓑ Tenzin and Dawa

They found the big rock where Tenzin had put his jar.

There was still some oil on the road, and it was slippery.

One of the men slipped in the oil.

He fell flat on his face.

He bumped into another man, who fell over, too.

One by one, all five men crashed down onto the road.

They lay there in a big heap. **Aha!**

"Get up!" groaned the man at the bottom of the heap.

"You are hurting me."

The first man got up.

He held onto the rock so that he would not fall again.

KEY WORDS

- slippery
- slip
- fall flat one's face
- another
- fall over
- one by one
- crash down
- in a big heap
- get up (get-got-gotten)
- groan
- at the bottom of
- hurt (hurt-hurt-hurt)
- hold onto (hold-held-held)

The second man got up.

He grabbed hold of the rock, too.

All five men got to their feet and tried to lift the rock.

"It is so heavy!" they gasped.

"How will we carry it back to the palace?"

They pulled and pushed.

But the rock did not move.

They pushed and pulled some more.

The rock moved a tiny bit.

At last, the five men lifted the heavy rock.

They carried it on their shoulders all the way back to the city.

When the five men reached the palace, they let the rock fall to the ground with a loud crash.

It was so heavy that the ground shook.

A crowd of people rushed out of their homes.

"Is it an earthquake?" they cried.

KEY WORDS

- grab hold of
- get to one's feet
- lift
- heavy
- gasp
- carry
- pull
- push
- move
- a tiny bit
- reach
- crash
- a crowd of
- rush out of
- earthquake

When they saw the rock, they laughed.

"Who put this rock here?

It belongs on the mountain road."

King Yeshi came out of the palace, and the people stopped laughing. **Aha!**

"Bring me the donkey," said the king.

"I will find out who broke the jar.

Was it the donkey's fault?

Or was the rock to blame?"

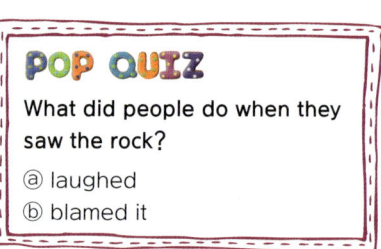

POP QUIZ

What did people do when they saw the rock?

ⓐ laughed
ⓑ blamed it

KEY WORDS

- laugh
- belong
- find out

- such a silly thing
- just
- living

- accident
- chew

The people laughed again.

"Who ever heard of such a silly thing?

A donkey is just an animal.

A rock is not a living thing.

It was nobody's fault.

The broken jar was just an accident."

But they all wanted to hear what the king was going to say.

The guard brought the donkey from the prison.

It stood next to the rock and chewed some hay.

"You all know that I cannot choose between the donkey and the rock," said the king.

The crowd agreed.

It was a foolish thing to do.

Was the king a fool after all?

"Then why have you all come to watch?" asked the king.

"You are the fools.

To teach you a lesson, you shall all pay me one coin before you leave." **Aha!**

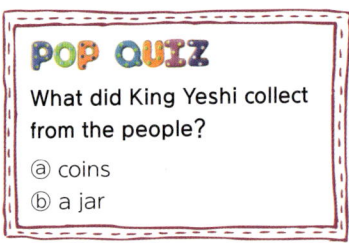

POP QUIZ

What did King Yeshi collect from the people?

ⓐ coins
ⓑ a jar

KEY WORDS

- choose
  (choose-chose-chosen)
- crowd
- foolish

- fool
- after all
- teach
  (teach-taught-taught)

- lesson
- coin
- enough
- thanks to

Each person paid the king.

King Yeshi gave all the coins to Tenzin.

Now he had enough money to buy food for his mother.

Tenzin and Dawa became friends thanks to wise King Yeshi.

Comprehension Quiz

A Who said what? Match each line with the right character(s).

 ❶

• • a) "I will find out who broke the jar."

 ❷

• • b) "Is it an earthquake?"

 ❸

• • c) "It is so heavy!"

B Match each word with its opposite.

❶ cry •   • a) foolish

❷ pull •   • b) light

❸ wise •   • c) laugh

❹ heavy •   • d) push

C What is NOT true about the five strong men?

❶ They fell down onto the slippery road.

❷ They had no money to feed their mothers.

❸ They found it hard to move the rock.

❹ They carried the rock on their shoulders.

D Solve the crossword puzzle with the right word that answers each question.

Across ❶ Who owned the donkey?

❷ Who owned the jar?

❸ What was the name of the king?

Down ❹ What animal was sent to prison?

❺ What was inside the jar?

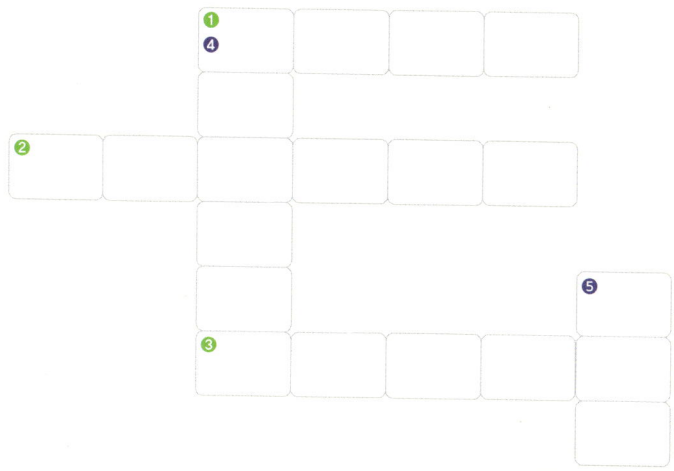

Stone Soup

Chapter One

The Man at the Door

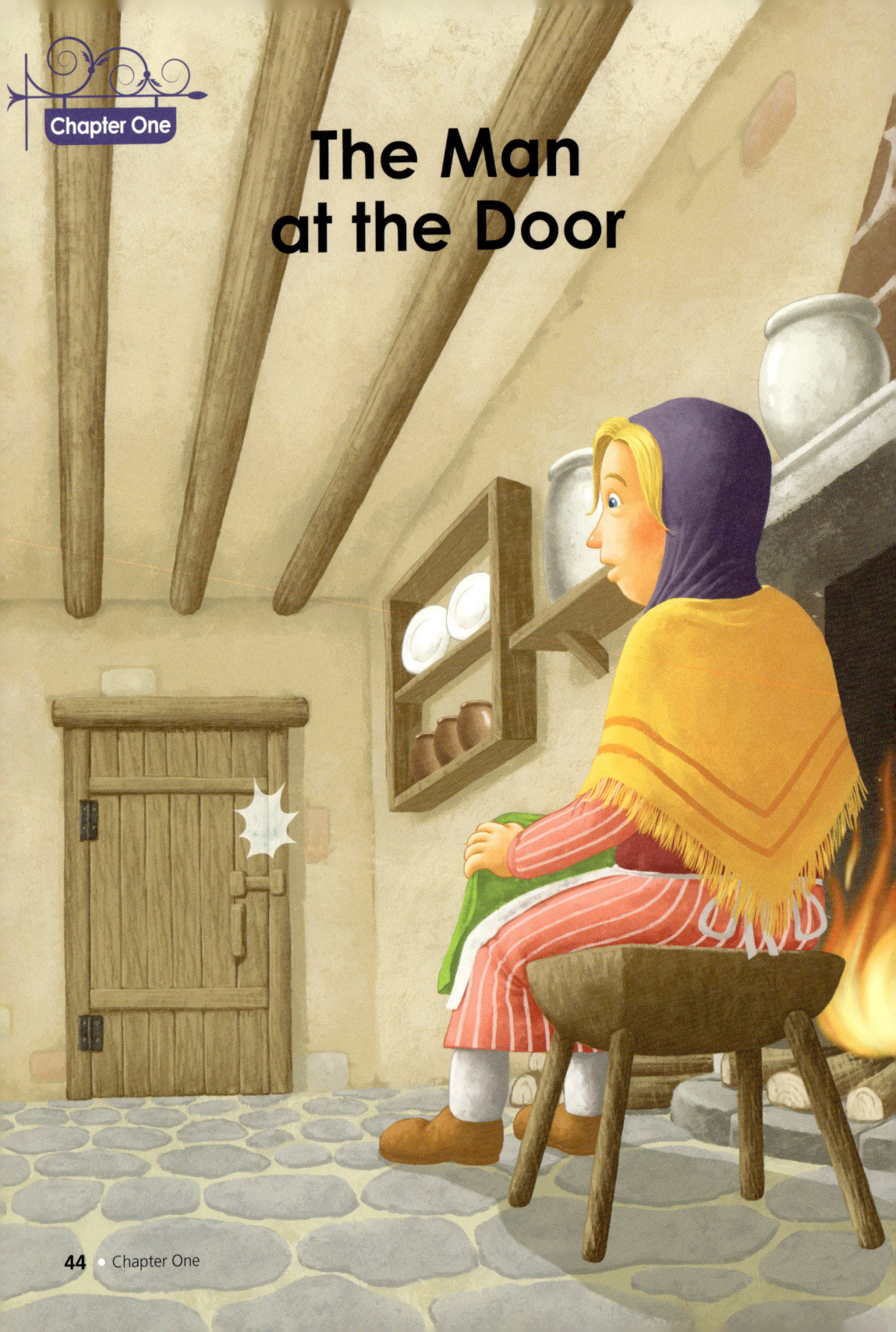

It was a dark, windy night in the middle of winter.

Snow blew against the door of the farmhouse.

The farmer's wife moved closer to the fire to keep warm. Aha!

Her husband, the farmer, was still out in the fields.

He had to take care of the sheep.

Suddenly, there was a knock at the door.

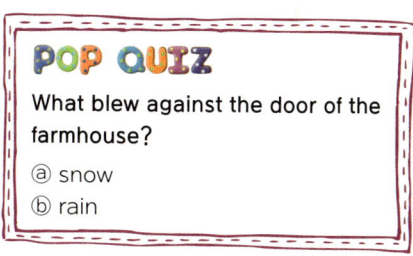

POP QUIZ

What blew against the door of the farmhouse?

ⓐ snow

ⓑ rain

KEY WORDS

- windy
- in the middle of
- **blow** (blow-blew-blown)
- against
- farmhouse
- closer
- **keep warm** (keep-kept-kept)
- out
- field
- suddenly
- knock

"Who's there?" called the farmer's wife.

"Is that you, husband?"

There was no answer.

The knock came again.

It was louder this time.

"Who's there?" called the farmer's wife again.

But only the wind howled at the window.

The farmer's wife pulled her shawl tight around her.

She picked up a stick and went to the door.

KEY WORDS

- answer
- louder
- howl
- shawl

- tight
- stick
- thin
- reply

- stranger
- glad
- look through
- crack

"Is anyone there?" she asked.

This time, a thin voice replied, "Open the door!"

"Who is it?" asked the farmer's wife.

She did not want to let a stranger in when her
husband was not at home.

"Just let me in," said the voice.

"You will be glad you did."

The farmer's wife opened the door a little.

She looked through the crack.

There was a man on the doorstep.

He looked thin and hungry.

"Please help me," he said.

"I have lost my way in the snow, and I am freezing."

The farmer's wife had a kind heart.

"Very well then," she said.

"But my husband and I are very poor.

I have no food to give you."

POP QUIZ

Where did the stranger stand?
ⓐ on the doorstep
ⓑ in the field

KEY WORDS

- doorstep
- lose one's way (lose-lost-lost)

- freeze (freeze-froze-frozen)
- very well then

"Then you need my magic soup stone," said the man. (Aha!)

He took a small, gray stone from his pocket. It looked like an ordinary stone.

It was the same as all the other stones in the farmyard.

"What is a soup stone?" said the farmer's wife.

"Let me show you," said the man.

▲ soup

KEY WORDS

- magic
- gray
- pocket

- look like
- ordinary
- the same as

- farmyard
- show

"You must fill a pot with water and boil it over the fire. Then, my stone will make the most delicious soup for you."
The farmer's wife was excited.
"Come in. Come in," she said.
"I must see how you make soup from a stone."

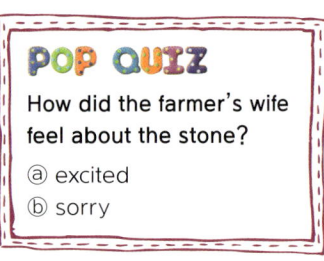

POP QUIZ
How did the farmer's wife feel about the stone?
ⓐ excited
ⓑ sorry

KEY WORDS

- fill
- pot
- boil
- delicious
- excited

- come in
- comfortable
- take off
- wet
- boot

- stretch
- toward
- hang (hang-hung-hung)

The man sat down in a comfortable chair.

He took off his wet boots and stretched his feet
toward the fire.

The farmer's wife filled a big pot with water.

She hung it over the fire, and it began to boil.

"What shall I do next?" she asked. Aha!

The man gave her the stone.

She dropped it into the water.

"Magic soup stone, make some soup!" said the man.

The farmer's wife looked into the pot.

"Nothing is happening," she said.

"You must stir it for a while," said the man.

"Stir and stir, but do not stop."

The farmer's wife took a wooden spoon and began to stir the water.

The man fell asleep in the chair and began to snore.

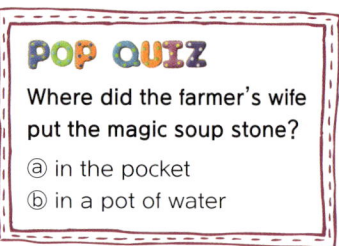

POP QUIZ

Where did the farmer's wife put the magic soup stone?

ⓐ in the pocket
ⓑ in a pot of water

KEY WORDS

- drop
- happen
- stir
- for a while

- snore
- wake up (wake-woke-woken)
- taste
- lick one's lips

"Wake up!" said the farmer's wife.

"The soup is boiling.

Shall we taste it now?"

The man woke up and licked his lips.

"That smells good," he said. Aha!

"The soup stone has made a good soup."

The farmer's wife could smell nothing.

The man leaned over the pot and dipped the spoon into the water.

The stone sat under the water at the bottom of the pot.

The man tasted the water and licked his lips.

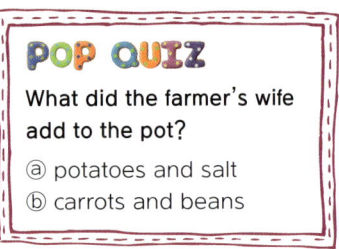

"The soup is delicious!" he said.

"But I think it needs a little bit of salt and some potatoes.

They will make it taste even better." Aha!

KEY WORDS

• lean over
• dip
• a bit of
• better

And he sat back in his chair and fell asleep once
more.

The farmer's wife got some potatoes.

She put them in the pot.

Then, she found some salt.

She put that into the pot, too.

"Magic soup stone, make some soup!" she said.

The farmer's wife sat by the fire.

She stirred the soup for a long time.

"Is it ready now?" she asked.

The man woke up with a jump.

He sniffed the air.

"It is almost ready," he said.

"The stone will make a good soup.

But it will be even better if we add some butter." Aha!

The farmer's wife jumped up.

She went to get some butter.

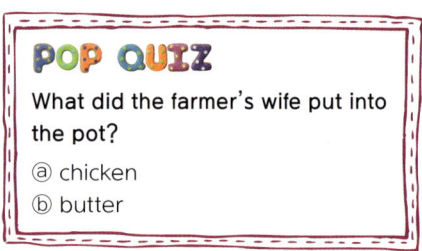

POP QUIZ

What did the farmer's wife put into the pot?

ⓐ chicken
ⓑ butter

KEY WORDS

- for a long time
- ready
- sniff

- almost
- add
- jump up

- vegetable

56 • Chapter One

"Put it in the pot," said the man.

She put the butter in the pot.

"Magic soup stone, make some soup!" said the man.

Then, he tasted the soup.

"It is delicious," he said.

"But a good soup like this needs some more vegetables.

Have you got some?"

"Oh, yes," said the farmer's wife.

She went to the cupboard and opened the door.

Inside the cupboard there were carrots and beans.

"Put the vegetables in the pot," said the man.

So the farmer's wife put the carrots and beans into the pot.

The man looked into the pot.

"Magic soup stone, make some soup!" he said.

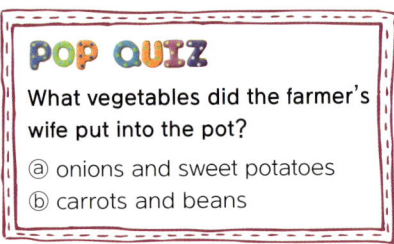

POP QUIZ

What vegetables did the farmer's wife put into the pot?

ⓐ onions and sweet potatoes
ⓑ carrots and beans

KEY WORDS

▪ cupboard   ▪ inside   ▪ or   ▪ work

"Can we eat it now?" asked the farmer's wife.

"I am very hungry."

"It is almost ready," said the man.

"You must keep stirring, or the soup stone will not work. Aha!

Stir and stir, and do not stop."

The farmer's wife stirred the soup with the big wooden spoon.

He sat back in the comfortable chair and smiled.

A Circle the right words to describe the magic soup stone.

a) gray

b) small

c) heavy

d) ordinary

e) black

B Circle the right word for each underlined part.

❶ The man on the doorstep was very (<u>cold</u> / <u>hot</u>).

❷ The man sat down and took off his (<u>boots</u> / <u>gloves</u>).

❸ The farmer's wife stirred the soup with a (<u>metal</u> / <u>wooden</u>) spoon.

❹ The man fell asleep in a (<u>chair</u> / <u>bed</u>).

C Choose the best answer to each question.

❶ Choose all the correct statements about the stranger.

a) He took care of the sheep.

b) He knocked at the door.

c) He tasted the soup.

d) He put salt in the pot.

❷ What was the last thing the farmer's wife did?

a) She let the man in.

b) She heard a knock.

c) She opened the door.

d) She picked up a stick.

D The man told the farmer's wife what to do. Choose the right word for each instruction.

open	boil	stir	fill

❶ _____ the door.

❷ _____ the pot.

❸ _____ the water.

❹ _____ the soup.

Soup for Supper

At last, the farmer's wife got tired of stirring the soup.

"It must be ready now!" she said.

"I am so hungry, and it smells so good."

The man stood up.

"It is almost ready," he said.

"The soup stone has done a good job.

But a delicious soup like this needs some chicken."

"You are right," said the farmer's wife.

"But the chickens are out in the chicken coop.

It is so cold outside.

I do not want to go out."

> **POP QUIZ**
>
> Why did the farmer's wife not want to go outside to get a chicken?
>
> ⓐ It was cold outside.
> ⓑ She was afraid of the chicken.

The man shook his head.

"Oh, dear," he said.

"The soup stone will not work if you are lazy.
You must get a chicken."

"You can get it," said the farmer's wife.

"Oh, no," said the man.

"I must stay and watch the soup stone, or the
magic will not work."

The farmer's wife put on her coat.

She opened the door.

Outside, it was dark and very cold.

But she did not want the soup stone to stop working.

So she went out to get a chicken for the pot.

Soon, she came back with a chicken.

She pulled all the feathers off and put it in the pot. 🔺

"Magic soup stone, make some soup!" she said.

"You must stir it," said the man.

"Stir and stir, and do not stop."

The farmer's wife stirred the soup.

KEY WORDS

- put on
- soon
- come back

- pull off
- feather

After a while, the chicken was cooked. Aha!

A delicious smell filled the room.

"It must be ready now," she said.

The man tasted the soup.

"Yes, it is ready.

Set the table."

The farmer's wife found some

bowls and spoons.

She put them on

the table.

The man sat

down and

waited for her

to serve him.

The farmer's wife put some of the soup into the bowls.

It was full of carrots, beans, potatoes, and butter.

Big pieces of chicken floated in the soup.

It tasted hot and salty.

It was the best soup the farmer's wife had ever tasted.

There was even some left over for her husband. Aha!

"The soup stone is really magic!" she gasped.

"May I keep it?"

"I am sorry," said the man.

"I need it.

There is no other stone like this in the world."

The pot was empty now.

Only the stone was at the bottom of it.

The man lifted the stone out of the pot and licked
it clean.

He did not look hungry anymore.

"Please come again tomorrow night," begged the

farmer's wife.

"Come for supper every night.

With your magic

soup stone, we

will never go

hungry again."

The man smiled

and licked his

lips.

"Thank you," he

said.

"I will do that."

The farmer's wife watched as the man walked away.

The farmyard was full of stones that looked just like the magic soup stone.

When the farmer came back, he was hungry.

"What is for supper?" he asked.

"It smells delicious."

"Soup," said the farmer's wife.

"A magic soup stone made it."

She told her husband all about the man and his stone.

The famer began to laugh.

He laughed and laughed.

KEY WORDS

▪ walk away

POP QUIZ

How did the farmer react after he heard about the magic soup stone?

ⓐ shouted
ⓑ laughed

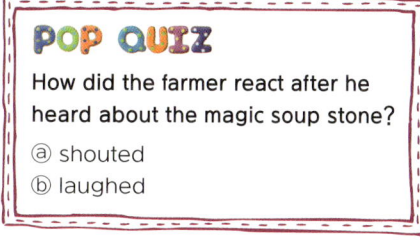

"The stone was not magic," he said.

"The soup tastes so good because it is full of chicken.  Aha!

There is salt and butter in it.

There are carrots, beans, and potatoes in it."

The farmer's wife began to laugh, too.

"It was a trick!" she said.

"I am such a fool."

"Never mind," said her husband.

"The soup was delicious, and the man is not hungry now."

"That's right," said the farmer's wife.

"And neither are we."

POP QUIZ

Why did the soup taste so good?

ⓐ because of the magic soup stone

ⓑ because it was full of chicken, salt, butter, carrots, beans, and potatoes

KEY WORDS

- trick
- Never mind.
- neither

Comprehension Quiz

 A Look at the word wall below. Check all the ingredients that were in the soup.

sugar	beef	potatoes
salt	flour	butter	water
tomatoes	chicken	bones
milk	beans	peas	carrots

B Mark T for true or F for false.

❶ The soup stone was really magic.　　　　T　F

❷ The man played a clever trick.　　　　T　F

❸ The man put his socks in the soup.　　　　T　F

❹ The farmer was angry with his wife.　　　　T　F

C Choose the best answer to each question.

❶ Why did the farmer's wife want to keep the soup stone?

a) She wanted to sell it and make money.

b) She wanted to make soup with it again.

c) She wanted to give it to her husband.

d) She wanted to throw it at the chickens.

❷ Where do you think the man got the soup stone?

a) from a magic shop

b) from a magician

c) from the farmyard

d) from his mother

D Circle the right word for each underlined part.

❶ The farmer's wife put on her (<u>coat</u> / hat).

❷ The man lifted the stone out of the (<u>pot</u> / bowl).

❸ The soup tasted (<u>salty</u> / sour).

❹ On the farm, there were (<u>cows</u> / <u>chickens</u>).

Let's Review the Story

Fill in the blanks to review the story.

❶ Title: Stories of _____

❷ Story 1: The _____ and the _____

❸ Place: A city in _____

❹ Main Characters: King Yeshi, Dawa, T_____

❺ Sequence:
1. Tenzin's jar breaks, and _____ spills out.
2. Tenzin and Dawa go to _____ to ask who is to blame.
3. Lots of _____ come to listen.
4. King Yeshi already knows it was an accident. He collects _____ from the people to pay for the oil.

❻ Story 2: _____ Soup

❼ Place: A farmhouse

❽ Main Characters: farmer's _____, stranger

❾ Sequence:
1. A hungry _____ goes to the farmer's wife.
2. He puts his magic soup _____ in a pot of water.
3. The _____ adds chicken, vegetables, and other things to the pot.
4. They eat the _____, and the stranger leaves. The stone is not _____ after all.

Let's Think & Talk

Think about the following questions and answer them freely.

❶ Think about how you would solve the problem if you were the king in "The Donkey and the Rock".

❷ If you were Dawa, the owner of the donkey that broke the oil jar, would you pay Tenzin, who asked to be paid, for the oil in the jar? Explain the reason.

❸ What kind of person is the strange man who brought the stone in "Stone Soup"? What makes you think that way?

❹ Tell us what you think about the strange man who cheated and lied to the farmer's wife.

Let's Review the Story

❶ Title: Stories of [Stone]

❷ Story 1: The [Donkey] and the [Rock]

❸ Place: A city in [Tibet]

❹ Main Characters: King Yeshi, Dawa, [Tenzin]

❺ Sequence:
1. Tenzin's jar breaks, and [oil] spills out.
2. Tenzin and Dawa go to [King Yeshi] to ask who is to blame.
3. Lots of [people] come to listen.
4. King Yeshi already knows it was an accident. He collects [coins] from the people to pay for the oil.

❻ Story 2: [Stone] Soup

❼ Place: A farmhouse

❽ Main Characters: farmer's [wife], stranger

❾ Sequence:
1. A hungry [stranger] goes to the farmer's wife.
2. He puts his magic soup [stone] in a pot of water.
3. The [farmer's wife] adds chicken, vegetables, and other things to the pot.
4. They eat the [soup], and the stranger leaves. The stone is not [magic] after all.

Smart Readers: **Wise & Wide**

After-reading Test

- Stories of Stone
- Level 2
- 19 Questions

   (Vocabulary 5 / Reading Comprehension 10 /

   Sentence Structure & Grammar 4)

1. Which of these words means "accident"?

   The broken jar was just an accident.

   ① something that is first made
   ② something that is broken
   ③ something that happens by chance
   ④ something that you keep oil in

2. Which pair has the wrong past tense form of the listed verb?
   ① leave – left
   ② grow – grew
   ③ come – comed
   ④ bring – brought

3. Which of the following does NOT have the similar meaning with the word "wise"?
   ① smart
   ② clever
   ③ kind
   ④ intelligent

4. Choose the right word for the blank.

   He had to take care _____ the sheep.

   ① of
   ② in
   ③ away
   ④ to

5. Which is NOT a pair of words that are opposites?
    ① open ↔ close
    ② foolish ↔ wise
    ③ hungry ↔ angry
    ④ poor ↔ rich

※ Choose the statement that does NOT match "The Donkey and the Rock". (6~7)
6. ① King Yeshi heard Tenzin and Dawa shouting.
    ② The guard gave the donkey some hay.
    ③ The five strong men fell over on the road.
    ④ The five strong men let the jar fall to the ground.

7. ① Dawa broke the jar of oil.
    ② The oil spilled onto the road.
    ③ The guard stood at the palace gate.
    ④ Tenzin put the oil into a jar.

8. Why did the people think there was an earthquake?
    ① They saw the rock.
    ② They heard it from King Yeshi.
    ③ The ground shook.
    ④ Their houses fell down.

9. Whose fault is the broken jar?
    ① It was the King Yeshi's fault.
    ② It was an accident.
    ③ It was the Dawa's fault.
    ④ It was the Tenzin's fault.

10. What did King Yeshi give Tenzin?
   ① donkey
   ② oil
   ③ coins
   ④ jar

11. Which word does NOT describe the background of the story "Stone Soup"?
   ① snowy
   ② cold
   ③ dark
   ④ bright

12. What is true about the stranger?
   ① He put salt in the pot.
   ② He went to fetch a chicken.
   ③ He licked the soup stone.
   ④ He laughed and laughed.

13. Which of the following is NOT related to the story "Stone Soup"?
   ① windy night
   ② hungry man
   ③ magic bowl
   ④ wooden spoon

14. What did the farmer's wife NOT say?
   ① "I must see how you make soup from a stone."
   ② "The soup stone will not work if you are lazy."
   ③ "The soup stone is really magic!"
   ④ "Please come again tomorrow night."

15. Which statement is NOT true?
   ① The farmer was out in the field.
   ② There were lots of stones in the farmyard.
   ③ The chickens were in the coop.
   ④ The carrots and beans weren't in the cupboard.

16. Choose the wrong part of the sentence.

   You must to pay me for the oil.
           ①   ② ③   ④

17. Choose the correct word for the blank.

   They will make it taste _____ better.

   ① more   ② even
   ③ too   ④ best

※ Choose the correct word or phrase for each blank. (18~19)
18.
   You must keep _____.

   ① stir   ② stirring
   ③ stirred   ④ to stir

19.
   After a while, the chicken _____.

   ① cooked   ② cooking
   ③ to cook   ④ was cooked

Memo

Memo

Memo

Memo

Sarah J. Dodd

Sarah J. Dodd is an experienced primary school teacher who resides in the UK, but has also taught in Australia. She has a PhD in Science and a certificate in Creative Writing. She has published four books for younger children — 'An Angel Anyway' (Anyway Press) and the Little Angels' series (Lion Hudson plc). Her children's Bible will be published in 2015. She is currently working on a novel for 9-12 year olds and another for young adults.

 Smart Readers **Wise & Wide** *2*-2

Stories of Stone

Retold by Sarah J. Dodd
Illustrated by Changjun Lee

First published December 2014
2nd printing October 2023

Publisher: Kyudo Chung
Editors: Juyon Choi, Jiyeong Park, Kyunghee Jang
Designer: Eunhee Lee

Published and distributed by
Happy House, an imprint of DARAKWON, Inc.
Darakwon Bldg., 211 Munbal-ro, Paju-si, Gyeonggi-do, 10881, Republic of Korea
Tel: 82-2-736-2031(Ext.250)   Fax: 82-2-732-2037   Homepage: www.ihappyhouse.co.kr

ISBN: 978-89-6653-161-5 18740 / 978-89-6653-156-1 18740(set)

[Components]
• Audio Files & Answer Keys & Korean Translation: Free download at www.ihappyhouse.co.kr

 This book is made with nontoxic materials.